HOW TO RUN
A MEETING

Harvard Business Review
CLASSICS

HOW TO RUN
A MEETING

Antony Jay

Harvard Business Press
Boston, Massachusetts

Copyright 2008 Harvard Business School Publishing Corporation

Originally published in *Harvard Business Review* in March 1976

Reprint #76204

Printed in the United States of America

13 12 11 10 09   5   4   3   2   1

Library-of-Congress cataloging information available

ISBN: 978-1-4221-4790-0

The paper used in this publication meets the requirements of the
American National Standard for Permanence of Paper for Publica-
tions and Documents in Libraries and Archives Z39.48-1992.

THE HARVARD BUSINESS
REVIEW CLASSICS SERIES

Since 1922, *Harvard Business Review* has
been a leading source of breakthrough ideas
in management practice—many of which still
speak to and influence us today. The HBR
Classics series now offers you the opportunity
to make these seminal pieces a part of your
permanent management library. Each volume
contains a groundbreaking idea that has
shaped best practices and inspired countless
managers around the world—and will change
how you think about the business world today.

{ v }

Why have a meeting anyway? Why indeed? A great many important matters are quite satisfactorily conducted by a single individual who consults nobody. A great many more are resolved by a letter, a memo, a phone call, or a simple conversation between two people. Sometimes five minutes spent with six people separately is more effective and productive than a half-hour meeting with them all together.

Certainly a great many meetings waste a great deal of everyone's time and seem to be held for historical rather than practical reasons; many long-established committees are little more than memorials to dead problems. It would probably save no end of managerial time if every committee had to discuss its own dissolution once a year, and put up a case if it felt it should continue for another twelve months. If this requirement did nothing else, it would at least refocus the minds of the committee members on their purposes and objectives.

But having said that, and granting that "referring the matter to a committee" can be a device for diluting authority, diffusing responsibility, and delaying decisions, I cannot deny that meetings fulfill a deep human need. Man is a social species. In every organization and every human culture of which we have record, people come together in small groups at regular and frequent intervals, and in larger "tribal" gatherings from time to time. If there are no meetings in the places where they work, people's attachment to the organizations they work for will be small, and they will meet in regular formal or informal gatherings in associations, societies, teams, clubs, or pubs when work is over.

This need for meetings is clearly something more positive than just a legacy from our primitive hunting past. From time to time, some technomaniac or other comes up with a vision of the executive who never leaves his home, who controls his whole operation from an all-electronic, multichannel, microwave, fiber-optic video display dream console in his living room. But any manager who has ever had to make an organization work greets this vision with a smile that soon stretches into a yawn.

There is a world of science fiction, and a world of human reality; and those who live in the world of human reality know that it is held together by face-to-face meetings. A meeting still performs functions that will never be taken over by telephones, teleprinters, Xerox copiers, tape recorders, television monitors, or any other technological instruments of the information revolution.

FUNCTIONS OF A MEETING

At this point, it may help us understand the meaning of meetings if we look at the six main functions that meetings will always perform better than any of the more recent communication devices.

In the simplest and most basic way, a meeting defines the team, the group, or the unit. Those present belong to it; those absent do not. Everyone is able to look around and perceive the whole group and sense the collective identity of which he or she forms a part. We all know who we are—whether we are on the board of Universal International, in the overseas sales department of Flexitube, Inc., a member of the school management committee, on the East Hampton football team, or in Section No. 2 of Platoon 4, Company B.

A meeting is the place where the group revises, updates, and adds to what it knows *as a group.* Every group creates its own pool of shared knowledge, experience, judgment, and folklore. But the pool consists only of what the individuals have experienced or discussed as a group—i.e., those things which every individual knows that all the others know, too. This pool not only helps all members to do their jobs more intelligently, but it also greatly increases the speed and efficiency of all communications among them. The group knows that all special nuances and wider implications in a brief statement will be immediately clear to its members. An enormous amount of material can be left unsaid that would have to be made explicit to an outsider.

But this pool needs constant refreshing and replenishing, and occasionally the removal of impurities. So the simple business of exchanging information and ideas that members have acquired separately or in smaller groups since the last meeting is an important contribution to the strength of the group. By questioning and commenting on new contributions, the group performs an important "digestive" process that extracts what's valuable and discards the rest.

Some ethologists call this capacity to share knowledge and experience among a group "the social mind," conceiving it as a single mind dispersed among a number of skulls. They recognize that this "social mind" has a special creative power, too. A group of people meeting together can often produce better ideas, plans, and decisions than can a single individual, or a number of individuals, each working alone. The meeting can of course also produce worse outputs or none at all, if it is a bad meeting.

However, when the combined experience, knowledge, judgment, authority, and imagination of a half dozen people are brought to bear on issues, a great many plans and decisions are improved and sometimes transformed. The original idea that one person might have come up with singly is tested, amplified, refined, and shaped by argument and discussion (which often acts on people as some sort of chemical stimulant to better performance), until it satisfies far more requirements and overcomes many more objections than it could in its original form.

A meeting helps every individual understand both the collective aim of the group and the way in which his own and everyone else's work can contribute to the group's success.

A meeting creates in all present a commitment to the decisions it makes and the objectives it pursues. Once something has been decided, even if you originally argued against it, your membership in the group entails an obligation to accept the decision.

The alternative is to leave the group, but in practice this is very rarely a dilemma of significance. Real opposition to decisions within organizations usually consists of one part disagreement with the decision to nine parts resentment at not being consulted before the decision. For most people on most issues, it is enough to know that their views were heard and considered. They may regret that they were not followed, but they accept the outcome.

And just as the decision of any team is binding on all the members, so the decisions of a meeting of people higher up in an organization carry a greater authority than any decision by a single executive. It is much harder to challenge a decision of the board than of the chief executive acting on his own. The decision-making authority of a meeting is of special importance for long-term policies and procedures.

In the world of management, a meeting is very often the only occasion where the team or group actually exists and works as a group, and the only time when the supervisor, manager, or executive is actually perceived as the leader of the team, rather than as the official to whom individuals report. In some jobs the leader does guide his team through his personal presence—not just the leader of a pit gang or construction team, but also the chef in the hotel kitchen and the maitre d'hôtel in the restaurant, or the supervisor in a department store. But in large administrative headquarters, the daily or weekly meeting is often the only time when the leader is ever perceived to be guiding a team rather than doing a job.

A meeting is a status arena. It is no good to pretend that people are not or should not be concerned with their status relative to the other members in a group. It is just another part of human nature that we have to live with. It is a not insignificant fact that the word *order* means (a) hierarchy or pecking order; (b) an instruction or command; and (c) stability and the way things ought to be, as in "put your affairs in order," or "law and order." All three definitions are aspects of the same idea, which is indivisible.

Since a meeting is so often the only time when members get the chance to find out their relative standing, the "arena" function is inevitable. When a group is new, has a new leader, or is composed of people like department heads who are in competition for promotion and who do not work in a single team outside the meeting, "arena behavior" is likely to figure more largely, even to the point of dominating the proceedings. However, it will hardly signify with a long-established group that meets regularly.

Despite the fact that a meeting can perform all of the foregoing main functions, there is no guarantee that it will do so in any given situation. It is all too possible that any single meeting may be a waste of time, an irritant, or a barrier to the achievement of the organization's objectives.

WHAT SORT OF MEETING?

While my purpose in this article is to show the critical points at which most meetings go wrong, and to indicate ways of putting them right, I must first draw some important distinctions in the size and type of meetings that we are dealing with.

Meetings can be graded by *size* into three broad categories: (1) the assembly—100 or more people who are expected to do little more than listen to the main speaker or speakers; (2) the council—40 or 50 people who are basically there to listen to the main speaker or speakers but who can come in with questions or comments and who may be asked to contribute something on their own account; and (3) the committee—up to 10 (or at the most 12) people, all of whom more or less speak on an equal footing under the guidance and control of a chairman.

We are concerned in this article only with the "committee" meeting though it may be described as a committee, a subcommittee, a study group, a project team, a working party, a board, or by any of dozens of other titles. It is by far the most common meeting all over the world, and can perhaps be traced back to the primitive hunting band through which our species evolved. Beyond doubt it constitutes the bulk of the 11 million meetings that—so it has been calculated—take place every day in the United States.

Apart from the distinction of size, there are certain considerations regarding the *type* of meeting that profoundly affect its nature. For instance:

Frequency—A daily meeting is different from a weekly one, and a weekly meeting from a monthly one. Irregular, ad hoc, quarterly, and annual meetings are different again. On the whole, the frequency of meetings defines—or perhaps even determines—the degree of unity of the group.

Composition—Do the members work together on the same project, such as the nursing and ancillary staff on the same ward of a hospital? Do they work on different but parallel tasks, like a meeting of the company's plant managers or regional sales managers? Or are they a diverse group—strangers to each other, perhaps—united only by the meeting itself and by a common interest in realizing its objectives?

Motivation —Do the members have a common objective in their work, like a football team? Or do they to some extent have a competitive working relationship, like managers of subsidiary companies at a meeting with the chief executive, or the heads of research, production, and marketing discussing finance allocation for the coming year? Or does the desire for success through the meeting itself unify them, like a neighborhood action group or a new product design committee?

Decision process—How does the meeting group ultimately reach its decisions? By a general consensus, "the feeling of the meeting"? By a majority vote? Or are the decisions left entirely to the chairman himself, after he has listened to the facts and opinions?

Kinds of Meetings

The experienced meeting-goer will recognize that, although there seem to be five quite different methods of analyzing a meeting, in practice there is a tendency for certain kinds of meetings to sort themselves out into one of three categories. Consider:

The *daily meeting,* where people work together on the same project with a common objective and reach decisions informally by general agreement.

The *weekly* or *monthly meeting,* where members work on different but parallel projects and where there is a certain competitive element and a greater likelihood that the chairman will make the final decision himself.

The *irregular, occasional,* or *"special project" meeting,* composed of people whose normal work does not bring them into contact and whose work has little or no relationship to the others'. They are united only by the project the meeting exists to promote and motivated by the desire that the project should succeed. Though actual voting is uncommon, every member effectively has a veto.

Of these three kinds of meetings, it is the first—the workface type—that is probably the most common. It is also, oddly enough, the one most likely to be successful. Operational imperatives usually ensure that it is brief, and the participants' experience of working side by side ensures that communication is good.

The other two types are a different matter. In these meetings all sorts of human crosscurrents can sweep the discussion off course, and errors of psychology and technique on the chairman's part can defeat its purposes. Moreover, these meetings are likely to bring together the more senior people and to produce decisions that profoundly affect the efficiency, prosperity, and even survival of the whole organization. It is, therefore, toward these higher-level meetings that the lessons of this article are primarily directed.

BEFORE THE MEETING

The most important question you should ask is: "What is this meeting intended to achieve?" You can ask it in different ways—"What would be the likely consequences of

not holding it?" "When it is over, how
shall I judge whether it was a success or a
failure?"—but unless you have a very clear
requirement from the meeting, there is a
grave danger that it will be a waste of everyone's time.

Defining the Objective

You have already looked at the six main
functions that all meetings perform, but if
you are trying to use a meeting to achieve
definite objectives, there are in practice only
certain types of objectives it can really
achieve. Every item on the agenda can be
placed in one of the following four categories, or divided up into sections that fall
into one or more of them.

Informative-digestive–Obviously, it is a waste of time for the meeting to give out purely factual information that would be better circulated in a document. But if the information should be heard from a particular person, or if it needs some clarification and comment to make sense of it, or if it has deep implications for the members of the meeting, then it is perfectly proper to introduce an item onto the agenda that requires no conclusion, decision, or action from the meeting, it is enough, simply, that the meeting should receive and discuss a report.

The "informative-digestive" function includes progress reports–to keep the group up to date on the current status of projects it is responsible for or that affect its deliberations—and review of completed projects in order to come to a collective judgment and to see what can be learned from them for the next time.

Constructive-originative—This "What shall we do?" function embraces all items that require something new to be devised, such as a new policy, a new strategy, a new sales target, a new product, a new marketing plan, a new procedure, and so forth. This sort of discussion asks people to contribute their knowledge, experience, judgment, and ideas. Obviously, the plan will probably be inadequate unless all relevant parties are present and pitching in.

Executive responsibilities—This is the "How shall we do it?" function, which comes after it has been decided what the members are going to do; at this point, executive responsibilities for the different components of the task have to be distributed around the table. Whereas in the second function the contributors' importance is their knowledge and ideas, here their contribution is the responsibility for implementing the plan. The fact that they and their subordinates are affected by it makes their contribution especially significant.

It is of course possible to allocate these executive responsibilities without a meeting, by separate individual briefings, but several considerations often make a meeting desirable.

First, it enables the members as a group to find the best way of achieving the objectives.

Second, it enables each member to understand and influence the way in which his own job fits in with the jobs of the others and with the collective task.

Third, if the meeting is discussing the implementation of a decision taken at a higher level, securing the group's consent may be of prime importance. If so, the fact that the group has the opportunity to formulate the detailed action plan itself may be the decisive factor in securing its agreement, because in that case the final decision belongs, as it were, to the group. Everyone is committed to what the group decides and is collectively responsible for the final shape of the project, as well as individually answerable for his own part in it. Ideally, this sort of agenda item starts with a policy, and ends with an action plan.

Legislative framework—Above and around all considerations of "What to do" and "How to do it," there is a framework—a departmental or divisional organization—and a system of rules, routines, and procedures within and through which all the activity takes place. Changing this framework and introducing a new organization or new procedures can be deeply disturbing to committee members and a threat to their status and long-term security. Yet leaving it unchanged can stop the organization from adapting to a changing world. At whatever level this change happens, it must have the support of all the perceived leaders whose groups are affected by it.

The key leaders for this legislative function must collectively make or confirm the decision; if there is any important dissent, it is very dangerous to close the discussion and make the decision by decree. The group leaders cannot expect quick decisions if they are seeking to change the organization framework and routines that people have grown up with. Thus they must be prepared to leave these items unresolved for further discussion and consultation. As Francis Bacon put it—and it has never been put better—"Counsels to which time hath not been called, time will not ratify."

Making Preparations

The four different functions just discussed may of course be performed by a single meeting, as the group proceeds through the agenda. Consequently, it may be a useful exercise for the chairman to go through the agenda, writing beside each item which function it is intended to fulfill. This exercise helps clarify what is expected from the discussion and helps focus on which people to bring in and what questions to ask them.

People

The value and success of a committee meeting are seriously threatened if too many people are present. Between 4 and 7 is generally ideal, 10 is tolerable, and 12 is the outside limit. So the chairman should do everything he can to keep numbers down, consistent with the need to invite everyone with an important contribution to make.

The leader may have to leave out people who expect to come or who have always come. For this job he may need tact; but since people generally preserve a fiction that they are overworked already and dislike serving on committees, it is not usually hard to secure their consent to stay away.

If the leader sees no way of getting the meeting down to a manageable size, he can try the following devices: (a) analyze the agenda to see whether everyone has to be present for every item (he may be able to structure the agenda so that some people can leave at half time and others can arrive); (b) ask himself whether he doesn't really need two separate, smaller meetings rather than one big one; and (c) determine whether one or two groups can be asked to thrash some of the topics out in advance so that only one of them needs to come in with its proposals.

Remember, too, that a few words with a member on the day before a meeting can increase the value of the meeting itself, either by ensuring that an important point is raised that comes better from the floor than from the chair or by preventing a time-wasting discussion of a subject that need not be touched on at all.

Papers

The agenda is by far the most important piece of paper. Properly drawn up, it has a power of speeding and clarifying a meeting that very few people understand or harness.

The main fault is to make it unnecessarily brief and vague. For example, the phrase "development budget" tells nobody very much, whereas the longer explanation "To discuss the proposal for reduction of the 1976–1977 development budget now that the introduction of our new product has been postponed" helps all committee members to form some views or even just to look up facts and figures in advance.

Thus the leader should not be afraid of a long agenda, provided that the length is the result of his analyzing and defining each item more closely, rather than of his adding more items than the meeting can reasonably consider in the time allowed. He should try to include, very briefly, some indication of the reason for each topic to be discussed. If one item is of special interest to the group, it is often a good idea to single it out for special mention in a covering note.

The leader should also bear in mind the useful device of heading each item "For information," "For discussion," or "For decision" so that those at the meeting know where they are trying to get to.

And finally, the chairman should not circulate the agenda too far in advance, since the less organized members will forget it or lose it. Two or three days is about right—unless the supporting papers are voluminous.

Other 'paper' considerations: The order of items on the agenda is important. Some aspects are obvious—the items that need urgent decision have to come before those that can wait till next ime. Equally, the leader does not discuss the budget for the re-equipment program before discussing whether to put the re-equipment off until next year. But some aspects are not so obvious. Consider:

- The early part of a meeting tends to be more lively and creative than the end of it, so if an item needs mental energy, bright ideas, and clear heads, it may be better to put it high up on the list. Equally, if there is one item of great interest and concern to everyone, it may be a good idea to hold it back for a while and get some other useful work done first. Then the star item can be introduced to carry the meeting over the attention lag that sets in after the first 15 to 20 minutes of the meeting.

- Some items unite the meeting in a common front while others divide the member one from another. The leader may want to start with unity before entering into division, or he may prefer the other way around. The point is to be aware of the choice and to make it consciously, because it is apt to make a difference to the whole atmosphere of the meeting. It is almost always a good idea to find a unifying item with which to end the meeting.

- A common fault is to dwell too long on trivial but urgent items, to the exclusion of subjects of fundamental importance whose significance is long-term rather than immediate. This can be remedied by putting on the agenda the time at which discussion of the important long-term issue will begin—and by sticking to it.

- Very few business meetings achieve anything of value after two hours, and an hour and a half is enough time to allocate for most purposes.

- It is often a good idea to put the finishing time of a meeting on the agenda as well as the starting time.

- If meetings have a tendency to go on too long, the chairman should arrange to start them one hour before lunch or one hour before the end of work. Generally, items that ought to be kept brief can be introduced ten minutes from a fixed end point.

- The practice of circulating background or proposal papers along with the minutes is, in principle, a good one. It not only saves time, but it also helps in formulating useful questions and considerations in advance. But the whole idea is sabotaged once the papers get too long; they should be brief or provide a short summary. If they are circulated, obviously the chairman has to read them, or at least must not be caught not having read them. (One chairman, more noted for his cunning than his conscientiousness, is said to have spent 30 seconds before each meeting going through all the papers he had not read with a thick red pen, marking lines and question marks in the margins at random, and making sure these were accidentally made visible to the meeting while the subject was being discussed.)

- If papers are produced at the meeting for discussion, they should obviously be brief and simple, since everyone has to read them. It is a supreme folly to bring a group of people together to read six pages of closely printed sheets to themselves. The exception is certain kinds of financial and statistical papers whose function is to support and illustrate verbal points as reference documents rather than to be swallowed whole: these are often better tabled at the meeting.

- All items should be thought of and thought about in advance if they are to be usefully discussed. Listing "Any other business" on the agenda is an invitation to waste time. This does not absolutely preclude the chairman's announcing an extra agenda item at a meeting if something really urgent and unforeseen crops up or is suggested to him by a member, provided it is fairly simple and straightforward. Nor does it preclude his leaving time for general unstructured discussion after the close of the meeting.

- The chairman, in going through the agenda items in advance, can usefully insert his own brief notes of points he wants to be sure are not omitted from the discussion. A brief marginal scribble of "How much notice?" or "Standby arrangements?" or whatever is all that is necessary.

THE CHAIRMAN'S JOB

Let's say that you have just been appointed
chairman of the committee. You tell everyone
that it is a bore or a chore. You also tell them
that you have been appointed "for my sins."
But the point is that you tell them. There is
no getting away from it: some sort of honor
or glory attaches to the chairman's role.
Almost everyone is in some way pleased and
proud to be made chairman of something.
And that is three quarters of the trouble.

Master or Servant?

Their appointment as committee chairman takes people in different ways. Some
seize the opportunity to impose their will

on a group that they see themselves licensed to dominate. Their chairmanship is a harangue, interspersed with demands for group agreement.

Others are more like scoutmasters, for whom the collective activity of the group is satisfaction enough, with no need for achievement. Their chairmanship is more like the endless stoking and fueling or a campfire that is not cooking anything.

And there are the insecure or lazy chairmen who look to the meeting for reassurance and support in their ineffectiveness and inactivity, so that they can spread the responsibility for their indecisiveness among the whole group. They seize on every expression of disagreement or doubt as a justification for avoiding decision or action.

But even the large majority who do not go to those extremes still feel a certain pleasurable tumescence of the ego when they take their place at the head of the table for the first time. The feeling is no sin: the sin is to indulge it or to assume that the pleasure is shared by the other members of the meeting.

It is the chairman's self-indulgence that is the greatest single barrier to the success of a meeting. His first duty, then, is to be aware of the temptation and of the dangers of yielding to it. The clearest of the danger signals is hearing himself talking a lot during a discussion.

One of the best chairmen I have ever served under makes it a rule to restrict her interventions to a single sentence, or at most two. She forbids herself ever to contribute a paragraph to a meeting she is chairing. It is a harsh rule, but you would be hard put to find a regular attender of her meetings (or anyone else's) who thought it was a bad one.

There is, in fact, only one legitimate source of pleasure in chairmanship, and that is pleasure in the achievements of the meeting—and to be legitimate it must be shared by all those present. Meetings are *necessary* for all sorts of basic and primitive human reasons, but they are *useful* only if they are seen by all present to be getting somewhere—and somewhere they know they could not have gotten to individually.

If the chairman is to make sure that the meeting achieves valuable objectives, he will be more effective seeing himself as the servant of the group rather than as its master. His role then becomes that of assisting the group toward the best conclusion or decision in the most efficient manner possible: to interpret and clarify; to move the discussion forward; and to bring it to a resolution that everyone understands and accepts as being the will of the meeting, even if the individuals do not necessarily agree with it.

His true source of authority with the members is the strength of his perceived commitment to their combined objective and his skill and efficiency in helping and guiding them to its achievement. Control and discipline then become not the act of imposing his will on the group but of imposing the group's will on any individual who is in danger of diverting or delaying the progress of the discussion and so from realizing the objective.

Once the members realize that the leader is impelled by his commitment to their common objective, it does not take great force of personality for him to control the meeting. Indeed, a sense of urgency and a clear desire to reach the best conclusion as quickly as possible are a much more effective disciplinary instrument than a big gavel. The effective chairman can then hold the discussion to the point by indicating that there is no time to pursue a particular idea now, that there is no time for long speeches, that the group has to get through this item and on to the next one, rather than by resorting to pulling rank.

There are many polite ways the chairman can indicate a slight impatience even when someone else is speaking–by leaning forward, fixing his eyes on the speaker tensing his muscles, raising his eyebrows, or nodding briefly to show the point is taken. And when replying or commenting, the chairman can indicate by the speed, brevity, and finality of his intonation that "we have to move on." Conversely, he can reward the sort of contribution he is seeking by the opposite expressions and intonations, showing that there is plenty of time for that sort of idea, and encouraging the speaker to develop the point.

After a few meetings, all present readily understand this nonverbal language of chairmanship. It is the chairman's chief instrument of educating the group into the general type of "meeting behavior" that he is looking for. He is still the servant of the group, but like a hired mountain guide, he is the one who knows the destination, the route, the weather signs, and the time the journey will take. So if he suggests that the members walk a bit faster, they take his advice.

This role of servant rather than master is often obscured in large organizations by the fact that the chairman is frequently the line manager of the members: this does not, however, change the reality of the role of chairman. The point is easier to see in, say, a neighborhood action group.

The question in that case is, simply, "Through which person's chairmanship do we collectively have the best chance of getting the children's playground built?"

However, one special problem is posed by this definition of the chairman's role, and it has an extremely interesting answer. The question is: How can the chairman combine his role with the role of a member advocating one side of an argument?

The answer comes from some interesting studies by researchers who sat in on hundreds of meetings to find out how they work. Their consensus finding is that most of the effective discussions have, in fact, two leaders: one they call a "team," or "social," leader; the other a "task," or "project," leader.

Regardless of whether leadership is in fact a single or a dual function, for our purposes it is enough to say that the chairman's best role is that of social leader. If he wants a particular point to be strongly advocated, he ensures that it is someone else who leads off the task discussion, and he holds back until much later in the argument. He might indeed change or modify his view through hearing the discussion, but even if he does not it is much easier for him to show support for someone else's point later in the discussion, after listening to the arguments. Then, he can summarize in favor of the one he prefers.

The task advocate might regularly be the chairman's second-in-command, or a different person might advocate for different items on the agenda. On some subjects, the chairman might well be the task advocate himself, especially if they do not involve conflict within the group. The important point is that the chairman has to keep his "social leadership" even if it means sacrificing his "task leadership." However, if the designated task advocate persists in championing a cause through two or three meetings, he risks building up quite a head of antagonism to him among the other members. Even so, this antagonism harms the group less by being directed at the "task leader" than at the "social leader."

Structure of Discussion

It may seem that there is no right way or wrong way to structure a committee meeting discussion.

A subject is raised, people say what they think, and finally a decision is reached, or the discussion is terminated. There is some truth in this. Moreover, it would be a mistake to try and tie every discussion of every item down to a single immutable format.

Nevertheless, there is a logical order to a group discussion, and while there can be reasons for not following it, there is no justification for not being aware of it. In practice, very few discussions are inhibited, and many are expedited, by a conscious adherence to the following stages, which follow exactly the same pattern as a visit to the doctor.

"What seems to be the trouble?" The reason for an item being on a meeting agenda is usually like the symptom we go to the doctor with: "I keep getting this pain in my back" is analogous to "Sales have risen in Germany but fallen in France." In both cases it is clear that something is wrong and that something ought to be done to put it right. But until the visit to the doctor, or the meeting of the European marketing committee, that is about all we really know.

"How long has this been going on?" The doctor will start with a case history of all the relevant background facts, and so will

the committee discussion. A solid basis of shared and agreed-on facts is the best foundation to build any decision on, and a set of pertinent questions will help establish it. For example, when did French sales start to fall off? Have German sales risen exceptionally? Has France had delivery problems, or less sales effort, or weaker advertising? Have we lost market share, or are our competitors' sales falling too? If the answers to all these questions, and more, are not established at the start, a lot of discussion may be wasted later.

"Would you just lie down on the couch?" The doctor will then conduct a physical examination to find out how the patient is now. The committee, too, will want to know

how things stand at this moment. Is action being taken? Do long-term orders show the same trend? What are the latest figures? What is the current stock position? How much money is left in the advertising budget?

"You seem to have slipped a disc." When the facts are established, you can move toward a diagnosis. A doctor may seem to do this quickly, but that is the result of experience and practice. He is, in fact, rapidly eliminating all the impossible or far-fetched explanations until he leaves himself with a short list. The committee, too, will hazard and eliminate a variety of diagnoses until it homes in on the most probable—for example the company's recent energetic and highly successful advertising campaign in Germany

plus new packaging by the market leader in France.

"Take this round to the druggist." Again, the doctor is likely to take a shortcut that a committee meeting may be wise to avoid. The doctor comes out with a single prescription, and the committee, too, may agree quickly on a single course of action.

But if the course is not so clear, it is better to take this step in two stages: (a) construct a series of options—do not, at first, reject any suggestions outright but try to select and combine the promising elements from all of them until a number of thought-out, coherent, and sensible suggestions are on the table; and (b) only when you have generated these options do you start to choose among them. Then you can discuss and decide whether to pick the course based on repackaging and point-of-sale promotion, or the one based on advertising and a price cut, or the one that bides its time and saves the money for heavier new-product promotion next year.

If the item is at all complex or especially significant, it is important for the chairman not only to have the proposed course of the discussion in his own head, but also to announce it so that everyone knows. A good idea is to write the headings on an easel pad with a felt pen. This saves much of the time wasting and confusion that result when people raise items in the wrong place because they were not privy to the chairman's secret that the right place was coming up later on in the discussion.

CONDUCTING THE MEETING

Just as the driver of a car has two tasks, to follow his route and to manage his vehicle, so the chairman's job can be divided into two corresponding tasks, dealing with the subject and dealing with the people.

Dealing with the Subject

The essence of this task is to follow the structure of discussion as just described in the previous section. This, in turn, entails listening carefully and keeping the meeting pointed toward the objective.

At the start of the discussion of any item, the chairman should make it clear where the meeting should try to get to by the end. Are the members hoping to make a clear decision or firm recommendation? Is it a preliminary deliberation to give the members something to go away with and think about? Are they looking for a variety of different lines to be pursued outside the meeting? Do they have to approve the proposal, or merely note it?

The chairman may give them a choice: "If we can agree on a course of action, that's fine. If not, we'll have to set up a working party to report and recommend before next month's meeting."

The chairman should make sure that all the members understand the issue and why they are discussing it. Often it will be obvious, or else they may have been through it before. If not, then he or someone he has briefed before the meeting should give a short introduction, with some indication of the reason the item is on the agenda; the story so far; the present position; what needs to be established, resolved, or proposed; and some indication of lines of inquiry or courses of action that have been suggested or explored, as well as arguments on both sides of the issue.

If the discussion is at all likely to be long or complex, the chairman should propose to the meeting a structure for it with headings (written up if necessary), as I stated at the end of the section on "Structure of discussion." He should listen carefully in case people jump too far ahead (e.g., start proposing a course of action before the meeting has agreed on the cause of the trouble), or go back over old ground, or start repeating points that have been made earlier. He has to head discussion off sterile or irrelevant areas very quickly (e.g., the rights and wrongs of past decisions that it is too late to change, or distant prospects that are too remote to affect present actions).

It is the chairman's responsibility to prevent misunderstanding and confusion. If he does not follow an argument or understand a reference, he should seek clarification from the speaker. If he thinks two people are using the same word with different meanings, he should intervene (e.g., one member using *promotion* to mean point-of-sale advertising only, and another also including media publicity).

He may also have to clarify by asking people for facts or experience that perhaps influence their view but are not known to others in the meeting. And he should be on the lookout for points where an interim summary would be helpful. This device frequently takes only a few seconds, and acts like a life belt to some of the members who are getting out of their depth.

Sometimes a meeting will have to discuss a draft document. If there are faults in it, the members should agree on what the faults are and the chairman should delegate someone to produce a new draft later. The group should never try to redraft around the table.

Perhaps one of the most common faults of chairmanship is the failure to terminate the discussion early enough. Sometimes chairmen do not realize that the meeting has effectively reached an agreement, and consequently they let the discussion go on for another few minutes, getting nowhere at all. Even more often, they are not quick enough to close a discussion *before* agreement has been reached.

A discussion should be closed once it has become clear that (a) more facts are required before further progress can be made, (b) discussion has revealed that the meeting needs the views of people not present, (c) members need more time to think about the subject and perhaps discuss it with colleagues, (d) events are changing and likely to alter or clarify the basis of the decision quite soon, (e) there is not going to be enough time at this meeting to go over the subject properly, or (f) it is becoming clear that two or three of the members can settle this outside the meeting without taking up the time of the rest. The fact that the decision is difficult, likely to be disputed, or going to be unwelcome to somebody, however, is not a reason for postponement.

At the end of the discussion of each agenda item, the chairman should give a brief and clear summary of what has been agreed on. This can act as the dictation of the actual minutes. It serves not merely to put the item on record, but also to help people realize that something worthwhile has been achieved. It also answers the question "Where did all that get us?" If the summary involves action by a member of the meeting, he should be asked to confirm his acceptance of the undertaking.

Dealing with the People

There is only one way to ensure that a meeting starts on time, and that is to start it on time. Latecomers who find that the meeting has begun without them soon learn the lesson. The alternative is that the prompt and punctual members will soon realize that a meeting never starts until ten minutes after the advertised time, and they will also learn the lesson.

Punctuality at future meetings can be wonderfully reinforced by the practice of listing late arrivals (and early departures) in the minutes. Its ostensible and perfectly proper purpose is to call the latecomer's attention to the fact that he was absent when a decision was reached. Its side effect, however, is to tell everyone on the circulation list that he was late, and people do not want that sort of information about themselves published too frequently.

There is a growing volume of work on the significance of seating positions and their effect on group behavior and relationships.

Not all the findings are generally agreed on.
What does seem true is that:

- Having members sit face to face across
  a table facilitates opposition, conflict,
  and disagreement, though of course it
  does not turn allies into enemies. But it
  does suggest that the chairman should
  think about whom he seats opposite.

- Sitting side by side makes disagree-
  ments and confrontation harder. This
  in turn suggests that the chairman can
  exploit the friendship-value of the seats
  next to him.

- There is a "dead man's corner" on the
  chairman's right, especially if a number

of people are seated in line along from him (it does not apply if he is alone at the head of the table).

- As a general rule, proximity to the chairman is a sign of honor and favor. This is most marked when he is at the head of a long, narrow table. The greater the distance, the lower the rank—just as the lower-status positions were "below the salt" at medieval refectories.

Control the Garrulous

In most meetings someone takes a long time to say very little. As chairman, your sense of urgency should help indicate to him

the need for brevity. You can also suggest
that if he is going to take a long time it might
be better for him to write a paper. If it is urgent to stop him in full flight, there is a useful device of picking on a phrase (it really
doesn't matter what phrase) as he utters it
as an excuse for cutting in and offering it to
someone else: "Inevitable decline—that's
very interesting. George, do you agree that
the decline is inevitable?"

Draw Out the Silent

In any properly run meeting, as simple
arithmetic will show, most of the people will
be silent most of the time. Silence can indicate general agreement, or no important
contribution to make, or the need to wait and

hear more before saying anything or too good a lunch, and none of these need worry you. But there are two kinds of silence you must break:

1. The silence of diffidence. Someone may have a valuable contribution to make but be sufficiently nervous about its possible reception to keep it to himself. It is important that when you draw out such a contribution, you should express interest and pleasure (though not necessarily agreement) to encourage further contributions of that sort.

2. The silence of hostility. This is not hostility to ideas, but to you as the

chairman, to the meeting, and to the process by which decisions are being reached.

This sort of total detachment from the whole proceedings is usually the symptom of some feeling of affront. If you probe it, you will usually find that there is something bursting to come out, and that it is better out than in.

Protect the Weak

Junior members of the meeting may provoke the disagreement of their seniors, which is perfectly reasonable. But if the disagreement escalates to the point of suggesting that they have no right to contribute, the meeting is weakened. So you may have to take pains to commend their contribution for its usefulness, as a pre-emptive measure. You can reinforce this action by taking a written note of a point they make (always a plus for a member of a meeting) and by referring to it again later in the discussion (a double-plus).

Encourage the Clash of Ideas

But, at the same time, discourage the clash of personalities. A good meeting is not a series of dialogues between individual members and the chairman. Instead, it is a crossflow of discussion and debate, with the chairman occasionally guiding, meditating, probing, stimulating, and summarizing, but mostly letting the others thrash *ideas* out. However, the meeting must be a contention of ideas, not people.

If two people are starting to get heated, widen the discussion by asking a question of a neutral member of the meeting, preferably a question that requires a purely factual answer.

Watch Out for the Suggestion-Squashing Reflex

Students of meetings have reduced everything that can be said into questions, answers, positive reactions, and negative reactions. Questions can only seek, and answers only supply, three types of responses: information, opinion, and suggestion.

In almost every modern organization, it is the suggestions that contain the seeds of future success. Although very few suggestions will ever lead to anything, almost all of them need to be given every chance. The trouble is that suggestions are much easier to ridicule than facts or opinions. If people feel that making a suggestion will provoke the negative reaction of being laughed at or squashed, they will soon stop. And if there is any status-jostling going on at the meeting, it is all too easy to use the occasion of someone's making a suggestion as the opportunity to take him down a peg. It is all too easy and a formula to ensure sterile meetings.

The answer is for you to take special notice and show special warmth when anyone makes a suggestion, and to discourage as sharply as you can the squashing-reflex. This can often be achieved by requiring the squasher to produce a better suggestion on the spot. Few suggestions can stand up to squashing in their pristine state: your reflex must be to pick out the best part of one and get the other committee members to help build it into something that might work.

Come to the Most Senior People Last

Obviously, this cannot be a rule, but once someone of high authority has pronounced on a topic, the less senior members are likely to be inhibited. If you work up the pecking order instead of down it, you are apt to get a wider spread of views and ideas. But the juniors who start it off should only be asked for contributions within their personal experience and competence ("Peter, you were at the Frankfurt Exhibition—what reactions did you pick up there?").

Close on a Note of Achievement

Even if the final item is left unresolved, you can refer to an earlier item that was well resolved as you close the meeting and thank the group.

If the meeting is not a regular one, fix the time and place of the next one before dispersing. A little time spent with appointment diaries at the end, especially if it is a gathering of five or more members, can save hours of secretarial telephoning later.

Following the Meeting

Your secretary may take the minutes (or better still, one of the members), but the minutes are your responsibility. They can be very brief, but they should include these facts:

- The time and date of the meeting, where it was held, and who chaired it.

- Names of all present and apologies for absence.

- All agenda items (and other items) discussed and all decisions reached. If action was agreed on, record (and underline) the name of the person responsible for the assignment.

- The time at which the meeting ended (important, because it may be significant later to know whether the discussion lasted 15 minutes or 6 hours).

- The date, time, and place of the next committee meeting.

ABOUT THE AUTHOR

Sir Antony Jay is former chairman of Video Arts Ltd., a London-based producer of training films for industry, and a distinguished broadcaster. He was the producer of a number of Queen Elizabeth II's Christmas broadcasts and was knighted for his work in public relations. This article springs from his research for a 1975 film on the subject of meetings (which featured John Cleese of Monty Python). He has also written many TV documentaries, such as *Royal Family*, and authored several books, including *Management & Machiavelli* (Holt, Reinhardt & Winston, 1968).

ALSO BY THIS AUTHOR

Harvard Business Review Article
"Rate Yourself as a Client," July 1977